SKYLANDERS UNIVERSE™

ULTIMATE
SEARCH-AND-FIND

GROSSET & DUNLAP
Published by the Penguin Group
Penguin Group (USA) LLC, 375 Hudson Street, New York, New York 10014, USA

ISBN 978-0-448-48059-6

10 9 8 7 6 5 4 3 2 1

INTRODUCTION

Welcome, young Portal Master. I am glad you have arrived. Something awful has happened. What's that? No, Flynn hasn't locked himself out of his cabin again. It's worse than that. The evil Kaos has cast a wicked spell upon the Portals of Power, and used them to scatter my most cherished magical instruments across the farthest corners of Skylands. I had thought they were in safe keeping with Hugo, but I'm afraid the poor Mabu is no match for such dark and powerful forces.

Now Kaos has sent his minions out to gather the lost items. If he gets them before you do, he will use them to inflict untold damage! I've already sent the Skylanders out to look for them—but they need your help to retrieve each artifact so that order can be restored.

Keep your eyes peeled, and good luck. All of Skylands is depending on you.

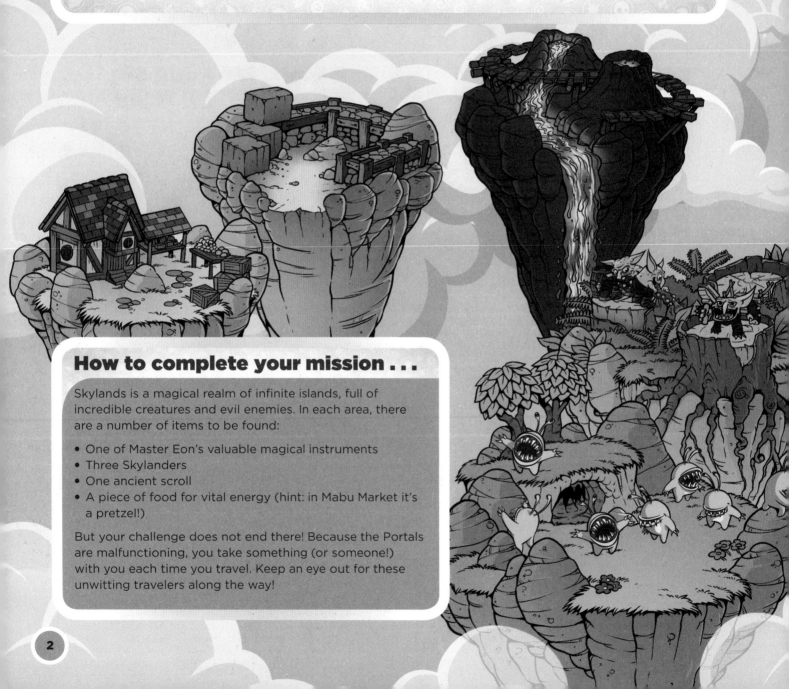

How to complete your mission . . .

Skylands is a magical realm of infinite islands, full of incredible creatures and evil enemies. In each area, there are a number of items to be found:

- One of Master Eon's valuable magical instruments
- Three Skylanders
- One ancient scroll
- A piece of food for vital energy (hint: in Mabu Market it's a pretzel!)

But your challenge does not end there! Because the Portals are malfunctioning, you take something (or someone!) with you each time you travel. Keep an eye out for these unwitting travelers along the way!

Completed your perilous quest? Turn to pages 28 to 31, where you will discover there is much, much more to Skylands than meets the eye!

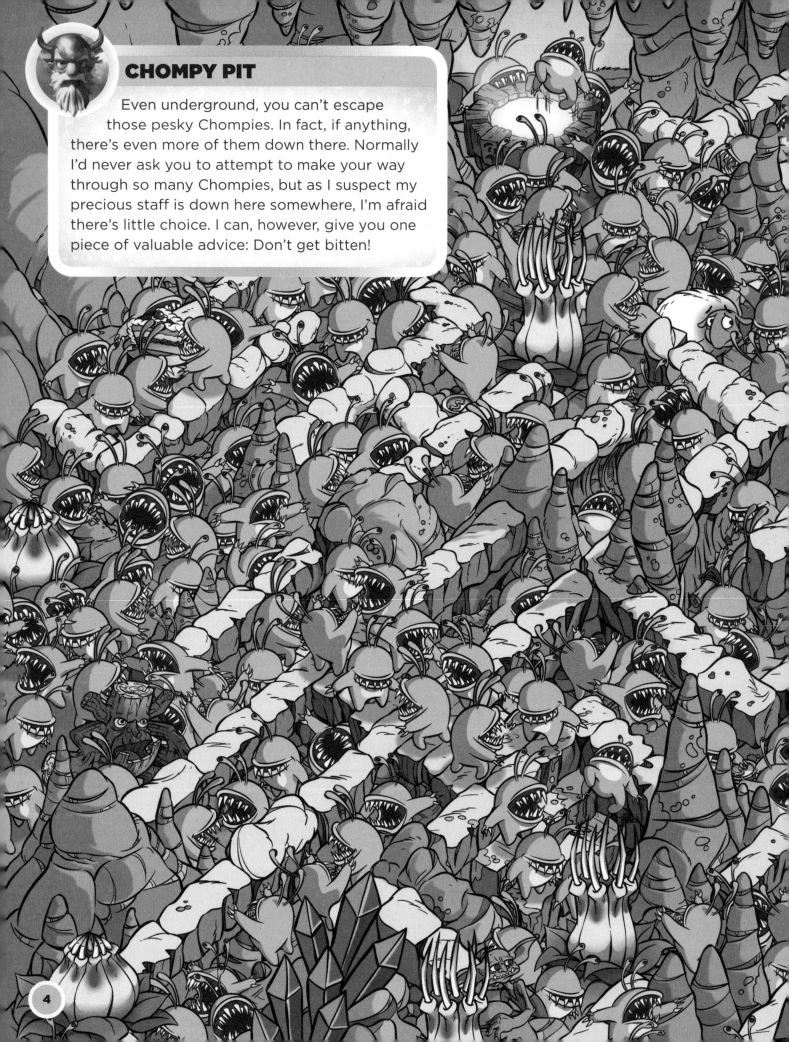

CHOMPY PIT

Even underground, you can't escape those pesky Chompies. In fact, if anything, there's even more of them down there. Normally I'd never ask you to attempt to make your way through so many Chompies, but as I suspect my precious staff is down here somewhere, I'm afraid there's little choice. I can, however, give you one piece of valuable advice: Don't get bitten!

DIRT BEACH

Terrafin was delighted to be sent to this popular tourist hot spot, for it reminds him of his former home—but this is no relaxing beach vacation. Dangers lurk both above and below the dunes, and believe me—getting all that sand out of your beard isn't exactly fun, either. You can work on your tan later. Now is the time to look for my abacus . . .

LAND OF THE UNDEAD

If you're faint of heart, weak of knee, or terrified of spiders, then this is probably not the place for you. Unfortunately, you have little choice but to venture down into this spooky, shadowy scene if you are to find my missing flask and complete the next chapter of your mission.

PLUNDER ISLAND

Pirates really make my beard bristle. They cheat, plunder, and generally make the place look thoroughly untidy. If it were up to me, they'd gather up their parrots, treasure chests, and shivering timbers, and sail off for good. I just hope you can find my cherished crystal ball before these salty sea dogs do.

FOREST OF FEAR

This is definitely not the sort of place you would want to take your dog for a quiet walk on a Sunday afternoon (sorry, Hot Dog). Here, eerie eyes peep out from behind every gnarled stump and twisted branch. So make like a tree and . . . well, I would say *leave*, but first you must track down my compass.

EMPIRE OF ICE

Tempting though it may be to engage in a snowball fight or build your very own snowgriffin, this is no time for messing around. There are more precious items to be found—starting with my magical antique ladle (which is occasionally used for dishing out magical antique soup).

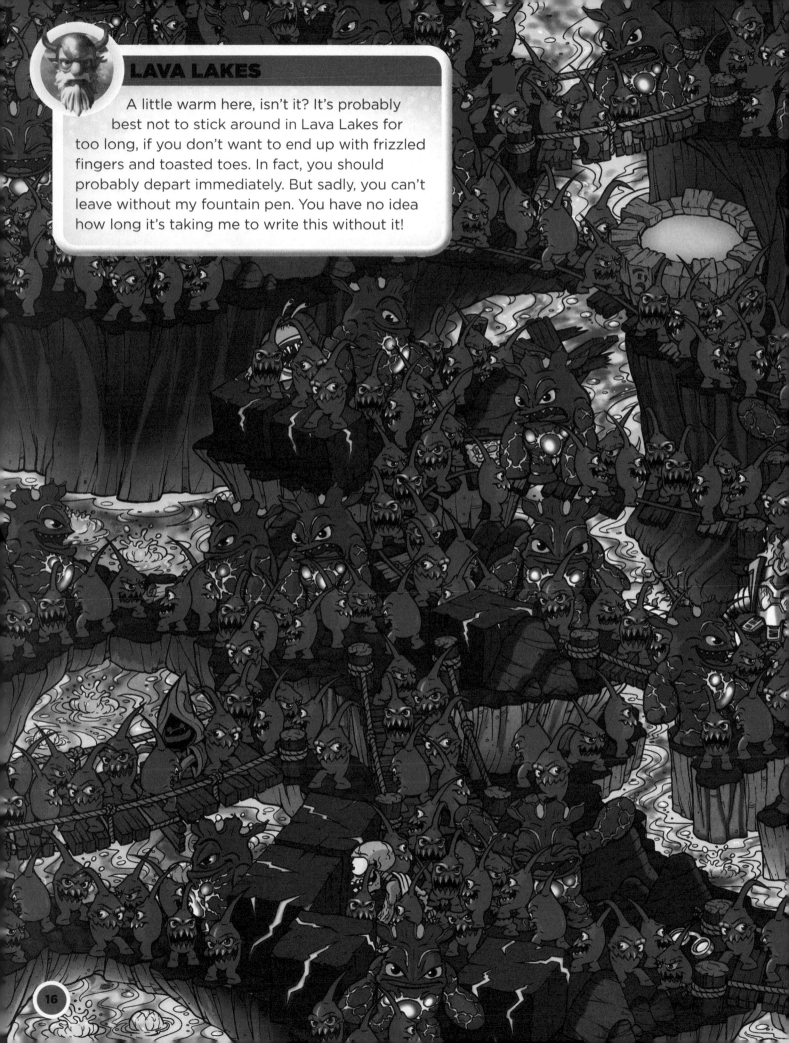

LAVA LAKES

A little warm here, isn't it? It's probably best not to stick around in Lava Lakes for too long, if you don't want to end up with frizzled fingers and toasted toes. In fact, you should probably depart immediately. But sadly, you can't leave without my fountain pen. You have no idea how long it's taking me to write this without it!

MABU MARKET

You can pick up some wonderful items at the Mabu Market. Indeed, I used to send Hugo here for my weekly supplies of fresh fruit and vegetables (until I met Camo, obviously). But you're not here to go shopping. Make your way through the bargain-hunting crowds, and recover my mystical ancient flute.

BENEATH STONETOWN

Skylands is full of ancient caverns and walkways, constructed many moons ago by our forefathers. One such place is this underground labyrinth, which is quite literally crawling with nocturnal knaves. Just look at them all! The keys to some of my citadel's oldest secrets have ended up down here somewhere. Can you find them?

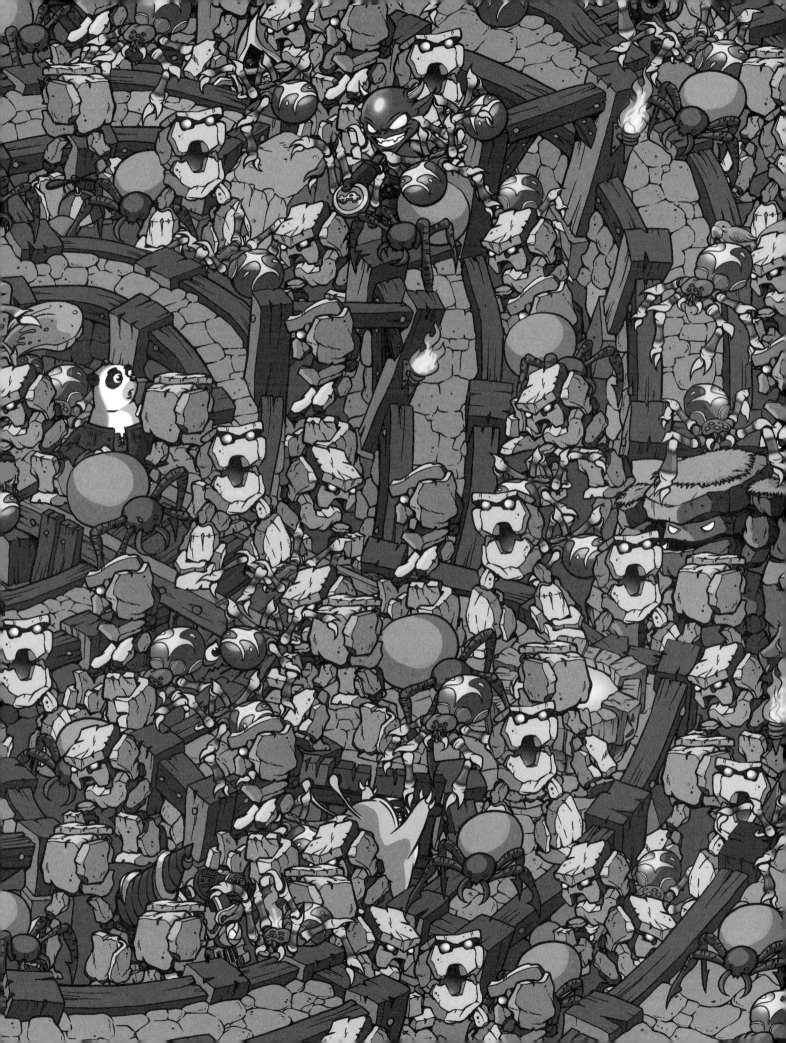

TURTLE ISLAND

So, young Portal Master, you have made it this far! I must say I am very, very impressed. But you cannot rest yet, for your toughest challenges are still ahead. Turtle Island, as you can see, has been overrun by watery villains. Somewhere among all this bedlam is my enchanted satchel, which can hold far more than it seems from the outside. I just hope it has not fallen into the water, for it could easily swallow up an entire sea.

GOLDSLINGER GULCH

You need to be pretty quick on the draw to make it through these parts—so it's a good thing Trigger Happy is around here somewhere. My undying candle has ended up here, too, so find it quickly. There's many a bandit, cowpoke, and sharpshooter who would love its eternal light to see them through those cold, starry desert nights.

KAOS'S KASTLE

And so, it comes to this: an encounter with my oldest (and might I say shortest) foe, Kaos. So far, you have managed to prevent him from getting his unusually small hands on some of Skylands' most important magical artifacts. But the most important treasure yet—my Skylands diary—is still to be found. It contains a colossal collection of observations made during my years as a Portal Master—and could be used by Kaos to cause catastrophic damage. Find it before he does!

Well done, Portal Master! You have completed your mission and restored peace to Skylands. The Skylanders and I cannot thank you enough. But of course, there are many, many other surprises to discover in our magical realm. Hop back on your Portal to return through the Skylands and see if you can spot any of these . . .

CHOMPY PIT Pages 4–5

- ◯ Hiding Glumshanks
- ◯ Rare Purple Chompy
- ◯ Worried sheep
- ◯ Onk's pencil
- ◯ Treasure chest
- ◯ Five gold coins
- ◯ Dino-Rang's stone boomerang

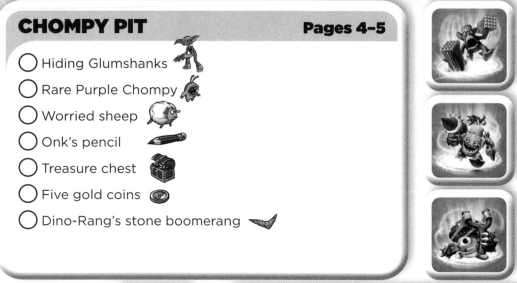

DIRT BEACH Pages 6–7

- ◯ Onk's writing pad
- ◯ Sheep wearing sunglasses
- ◯ Evil eyes looking out from a sand castle
- ◯ Lost Chompy
- ◯ Fez hat
- ◯ Flameslinger's bow and arrow

LAND OF THE UNDEAD Pages 8–9

- ◯ Undead sheep
- ◯ Lost Chompy
- ◯ Lost young troll in swimming trunks and armbands
- ◯ Santa hat
- ◯ Boomer's sticks of dynamite

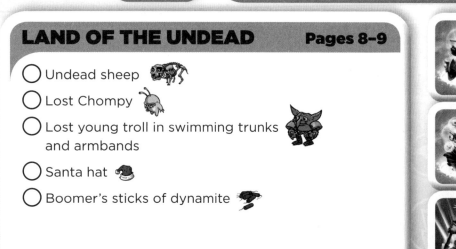

PLUNDER ISLAND   Pages 10–11

- ○ Four gold coins
- ○ Two pirates playing Skystones
- ○ Sheep in a pirate hat
- ○ Lost Chompy
- ○ Lost young troll in swimming trunks and armbands
- ○ Lost Rotting Robbie
- ○ Anvil hat
- ○ Voodood's Axe Reaver

FOREST OF FEAR   Pages 12–13

- ○ Camouflaged dragon's egg
- ○ Sheep chewing on a twig
- ○ Lost Chompy
- ○ Lost young troll in swimming trunks and armbands
- ○ Lost Rotting Robbie
- ○ Lost pirate parrot
- ○ Viking helmet
- ○ Double Trouble's staff

EMPIRE OF ICE   Pages 14–15

- ○ Young cyclops in a scarf pulling a sled along
- ○ Sheep in a woolly hat and scarf
- ○ Lost Chompy
- ○ Lost young troll in swimming trunks and armbands
- ○ Lost Rotting Robbie
- ○ Lost pirate parrot
- ○ Lost Life Spell Punk
- ○ Top hat
- ○ Sprocket's wrench

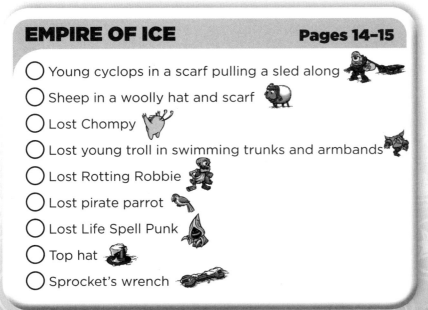

LAVA LAKES

Pages 16–17

- ◯ Flame Imp taking a nap
- ◯ Sheep wearing a welding helmet
- ◯ Lost Chompy
- ◯ Lost young troll in swimming trunks and armbands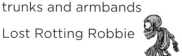
- ◯ Lost Rotting Robbie
- ◯ Lost pirate parrot
- ◯ Lost Life Spell Punk
- ◯ Lost snowman
- ◯ Chef's hat
- ◯ Hugo's glasses

MABU MARKET

Pages 18–19

- ◯ Mabu holding up a fish
- ◯ Annoyed sheep being used as a table
- ◯ Lost Chompy
- ◯ Lost young troll in swimming trunks and armbands
- ◯ Lost Rotting Robbie
- ◯ Lost pirate parrot
- ◯ Lost Life Spell Punk
- ◯ Lost snowman
- ◯ Lost Flame Imp
- ◯ Jester hat
- ◯ Spine from Warnado's shell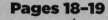

BENEATH STONETOWN

Pages 20–21

- ◯ Hob 'n' Yaro clutching a gold coin
- ◯ Sheep covered in dust
- ◯ Lost Chompy
- ◯ Lost young troll in swimming trunks and armbands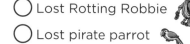
- ◯ Lost Rotting Robbie
- ◯ Lost pirate parrot
- ◯ Lost Life Spell Punk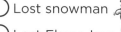
- ◯ Lost snowman
- ◯ Lost Flame Imp
- ◯ Lost Mabu market-stall owner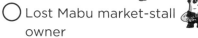
- ◯ Propeller cap
- ◯ Wham-Shell's Malacostracan Mace

TURTLE ISLAND

Pages 22–23

- ⃝ Turtle with its head inside its shell
- ⃝ Sheep wearing a snorkel
- ⃝ Lost Chompy
- ⃝ Lost young troll in swimming trunks and armbands
- ⃝ Lost Rotting Robbie
- ⃝ Lost pirate parrot
- ⃝ Lost Life Spell Punk
- ⃝ Lost snowman
- ⃝ Lost Flame Imp
- ⃝ Lost Mabu market-stall owner
- ⃝ Lost Spider Swarmer
- ⃝ Tiki hat
- ⃝ Camo's favorite exploding watermelon

GOLDSLINGER GULCH

Pages 24–25

- ⃝ Cactus with no spines
- ⃝ Sheep wearing a cowboy hat and sheriff's badge
- ⃝ Lost young troll in swimming trunks and armbands
- ⃝ Lost Rotting Robbie
- ⃝ Lost pirate parrot
- ⃝ Lost Life Spell Punk
- ⃝ Lost snowman
- ⃝ Lost Flame Imp
- ⃝ Lost Mabu market-stall owner
- ⃝ Lost Spider Swarmer
- ⃝ Lost blowfish
- ⃝ Plunger head hat
- ⃝ Chop Chop's sword

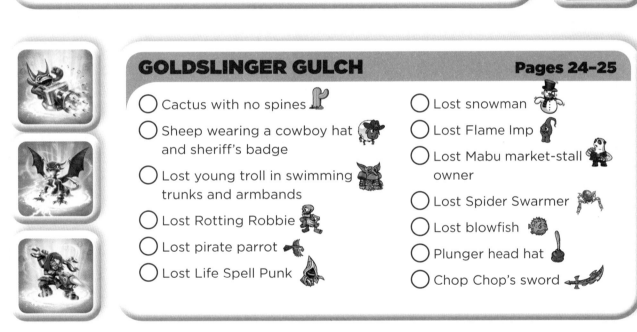

KAOS'S KASTLE

Pages 26–27

- ⃝ Drow Spearman who has accidentally speared a fellow Drow Spearman in the rear end
- ⃝ Sheep wearing a soldier's helmet
- ⃝ Lost young troll in swimming trunks and armbands
- ⃝ Lost Rotting Robbie
- ⃝ Lost pirate parrot
- ⃝ Lost Life Spell Punk
- ⃝ Lost snowman
- ⃝ Lost Flame Imp
- ⃝ Lost Mabu market stall-owner
- ⃝ Lost Spider Swarmer
- ⃝ Lost blowfish
- ⃝ Lost cactus
- ⃝ Wabbit Ears hat
- ⃝ Ghost Roaster's ball and chain

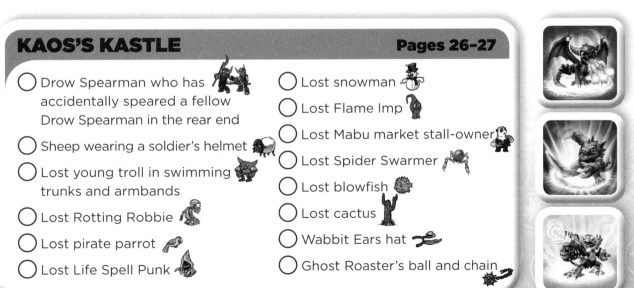